The Indigo Child's Survival Guide

The Indigo Child's Survival Guide
Unlock your Super Natural Powers & Thrive as an Indigo Child

Written by:
Baker, with Sim1 Indigo and Mama Indigo

Copyright 2012-2015. © Baker, Sim1 Indigo and Mama Indigo. All Rights Reserved. No part of this publication may be reproduced or sold in any form, except by written consent of the author(s)

Published by Virgo eBooks Publishing LLC
www.virgoebooks.com
Vermont / New York
2015

Second edition – January 2015

ISBN 13: 978-1478397960
ISBN 10: 1478397969

Disclaimer: Each story and technique described in this book is based on real-life personal experiences that the authors have worked with directly and that have helped them personally. The authors do not claim to be trained professional medical doctors. The authors of this book are not responsible for any medical related, or health related issues that you may have. If you are having any conditions that require serious medical attention consult a health professional immediately.

Contents

Chapter 1. What is an Indigo Child? 7
Chapter 2. How can you tell if you are an Indigo? 12
Chapter 3. Problems and Solutions for Indigos 14
Clearing Negative Energy From You As a Sensitive Indigo 14

The Color Choices of the Light 17

Energetic Cleansing Techniques 19

Centering and Grounding for the Indigo Child 23

Energy Healing 27

Chapter 4. Psychic Abilities 33
Chapter 5. Receiving Guidance – Guides and Messengers 38
Animals as Messengers and Guides 45

Synchronicity 48

Chapter 6. How to Find and Follow Your Passion as an Indigo Child 51
Chapter 7. Manifest Your Desires as an Indigo Child 57
Creative Visualization in Practice 64

Chapter 8. Make Your Everyday Life a Meditation 66
Dance as Movement Meditation and Spiritual Practice 70

Chapter 9. Empathy 101: A Basic Understanding of Feeling Others Emotions 81
Chapter 10. Psychic Training 92
Chapter 11. Raising and Mentoring New Paradigm Kids 100
Chapter 12. This Is Only the Beginning 106
About the Authors 114
Baker's Bio 114

Mama Indigo's Bio 116

Sim1's Bio 118

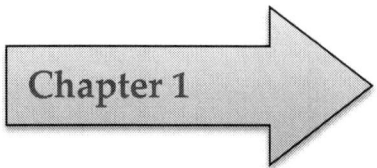
Chapter 1

What is an Indigo Child?

There really isn't one definitive answer. In simple terms it is a person with a warrior spirit, always questioning and challenging the ways of the world and has a strong sense of a higher purpose. Some texts say that Indigo Children are born in a certain year. I don't believe that you can classify Indigo Children into the decade or year they were born. Being an Indigo Child is more about being at a certain level of consciousness. The Indigo Child may show signs of supernatural powers like feeling others' emotions, visions, and healing (the technical terms will be discussed later in the book). The possibilities of these gifts of the mind are infinite; believing in and accepting yourself as an Indigo is the key. Indigo is a label humans created to identify a group of people who have opened their minds beyond what is said by society to be "normal." The name Indigo Child is the gateway that leads you to more answers. The Indigo Child is what I like to call the "system-busters" of our society. They share a collective mission of taking down old, outdated, negative, fear-based, ego-dominated structures and lower conscious related systems to make room for creating a world of peace, harmony, and love for humanity and for future generations to come.

However, the best way for me to explain more would be to share with you some of my own personal experiences as an Indigo and provide some insight into some of the topics covered in this book. The purpose of this book is to help those seeking guidance; something I wish I had when I was beginning to figure out who I was and what I was capable of becoming.

My whole life I have always felt that I was put here for something really important. One-in-a-million freak accidents seemed to always happen to me starting with the day I was born and well into my adult years, which I would miraculously survive with little to no injury. I received good grades in school but with a constant reprimand of my misbehavior. I rebelled against authority. Always wanted to know "why" and "because I said so," certainly wasn't an acceptable answer. I remember being spanked as punishment for whatever it was I did wrong and often the paddle was busted on me because I wouldn't cry immediately. I still do not understand where this is justified or a lesson learned. I stared at trees and the stars often and always felt a strong connection to animals and nature.

What I did discover at an early age was that I had the talent to help people find reasons to smile, which was when I wasn't defying them. I do not remember exactly when my "gifts" began to emerge. I noticed the emotional roller coaster I was on was an extension of what the people around me were feeling. I knew who was calling whenever the phone rang. I would get pictures in my mind of people and places I didn't know. I also noticed that when I really wanted something, in strange ways I always got what I asked for; I now know this is the Law of Attraction (discussed in later chapters of this book). When I attempted to discuss these experiences with my devoted Christian parents I was often told that I was crazy and "getting too far out there." Without the guidance I was seeking, I retreated into myself.

As I grew older, I never let go of that feeling that I was meant for something big. I analyzed everything. Every school lesson, religion, the government, the way people behaved; in general, how the world worked. I noticed more and more moments that felt like they had already happened (déja vu). I'd watch the news, knowing it's not the whole truth and would get a theorized mini-movie in my mind (could be the truth).

I would visualize my entire home and the contents to locate an item that I seemed to have lost; and visually see it in a box in the closet. And that is where I would physically find it. I would hold an object and feel the energy in it and in my mind I would see part of its history. I saw ghosts in a couple of homes I had lived in which freaked me out a little because I was raised being told they were evil. I had conversations with a friend in our minds while sitting next to each other, never speaking a word, but confirmed it with each other later. I knew I wasn't "crazy." I knew these gifts were real. What I didn't know was who to talk to about it without the fear of being told that I was wrong and it wasn't real.

When the student is ready, the teacher will appear… It was when I began to do yard work for a new friend that I was introduced to Wicca, something I was raised being told was evil. This friend taught me about meditation, the chakras, centering myself, how to speak to animals, healing, and helped me refine and control the visions and empathy gifts. Wow! I was so thrilled to finally have some guidance from someone that believed in the experiences I was already having. It was a new beginning for my life that I struggled with for so long. Eventually, I began to follow my own path; Wicca was cool but still did not completely resonate with me. I kept searching for more answers. I honestly do not remember how I came across the term Indigo Child. But once I did, a whole new world opened up. I made many new friends who had similar life experiences as I did. I learned that these mind powers I had were only the beginning. The possibilities, what our minds, our spirits are entirely capable of, are infinite. Not only did I learn more, I began to teach younger generations of Indigo Children. The more I teach, the more I learn about myself. And the more I learn about myself, the more I am able to share with others who are willing to listen.

I sincerely hope you will find the information in this book helpful. Those of us who yearned for some answers as we were growing up decided to create some sort of survival guide for the Indigo Child in an effort to assist you with your own daily struggle in this 3 dimensional world. The important thing to remember is that everyone is different. A technique that works for some may not work for others. Each of us has a mission, a purpose... what are you supposed to do? Refine and master your gifts. Use the techniques in this book to help you protect yourself from the dark side, and further assist you to unlock your supernatural powers and thrive as an Indigo Child. ALWAYS THINK AND SPEAK POSITIVE! Learn the lessons the universe puts in front of you, quickly. And remember that karma and the Law of Attraction are very real. LIVE. LOVE. LAUGH.

www.mamaindigo.blogspot.com

"**Mama Indigo**"

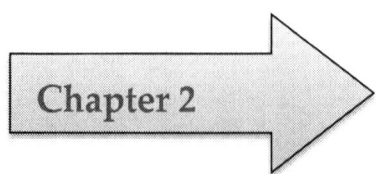

How can you tell if you are an Indigo?

A good way to "test" yourself is to answer the following questions:

1. Do you sometimes feel a lot wiser beyond your years?
2. Do you feel alone or isolated in your beliefs?
3. Do you have trouble conforming to the ways of society?
4. Are you a seeker of truth?
5. Do you feel out of place in today's society?
6. Do you have stronger intuition about certain things that most do not?
7. Do you often feel misunderstood when you try to talk to people about what's real?
8. Are you always searching for your greater purpose in life but feel like the world isn't set up for you?
9. Do you feel like you were born to accomplish a special mission in life?
10. Are you easily misunderstood by your family (parents, uncles, aunts)?
11. Do you feel shy or withdrawn unless you are with people of like mind?

12. Do you perceive the world a lot differently than most people around you?

13. Are you emotionally sensitive person?

14. Did you have a difficult Childhood compared to other people?

15. Do you often feel disempowered by being around too much authority?

If you can answer yes to many of these questions, then you are most likely an Indigo.

So what now? I took the test I'm an Indigo. The next chapter will cover the problems and solutions for Indigos living today.

Chapter 3

Problems and Solutions for Indigos

Clearing Negative Energy From You As a Sensitive Indigo

One of the topics people seek advice about most often with me is in regards to psychic energy protection. As an Indigo, you may be very sensitive to any energies all around you. It can become overwhelming and at times even drain us.

To prevent this from happening, it is helpful to have some techniques on hand to protect you against any negative energy or energy drains.

You may also want to find ways to discern between thoughts or feelings that originate from someone else versus your own. This takes practice and the signs are subtle. It feels different than coming from you, a different sensation. Ask for divine guidance when in doubt.

Some people may choose to use crystal or other protective charms to help shield them from the influx of energies. However, there are many techniques you can use when you do not have anything on hand, something you can do to protect yourself energetically and also cleanse yourself if you have done an energy healing.

I am putting cleanses and protections into one section as once you are experiencing someone else's energy, you usually want to get rid of it again.

The first technique is a visualization of a light shield in the form of a vortex bubble surrounding your auric field and physical body. This bubble can protect you against psychic attacks and against humans that subconsciously may try to leach from others (energy vampires). This may also help any empath that feel the energy of anyone around them.

Imagine a cylinder/vortex of bright light surrounding your energy and physical body. The source of the light may come from above and/or below, enveloping you and your energy field completely from top to bottom.

It is important that you enforce this energetic light shield through your intentions and prayers to keep out all negativity. Use affirmations such as: "May only positive energy, thoughts, love and compassion pass this boundary. No one may tap into my energy unless I give permission to do so."

The source where the light comes from can either be from above (heaven, cosmos, Universe, the Divine/Spirit/God, from the earth, or from above and below.

Some start the light vortex protection shield from their light within, from their Hara center, which is about half an inch below your navel. You may imagine a strongly burning ball of light, expanding outwards until it surrounds your energy field completely. You fuel it with your intentions.

If you are an empath, and in a group of people, I suggest to bring in your energy field as close as you can to your physical body. Empaths' heart energy fields tend to extend far outside their aura energy field and therefore can easily detect and take on other people's energies and feelings. If you envision the light bubble/your energy field around you snug and tight like a white light blanket wrapped around your body, it should help you to not pick up other people's energy fields.

The Color Choices of the Light

I will add a section about the choice of color you may visualize your light as. There are some colors that are most frequently used for protective light energy: gold, white and blue. I am quoting a section of David Furlong's article on colors and their meaning. You can experiment with either one and use the color working best for you:

"Gold is associated with the sun and carries a powerful Yang, or positive energy that can be very forceful. It will consume any energy that is not in harmony with it. Those who have an outgoing, positive outlook on life will find this energy most appropriate. It suits the action people of this world. It is a color that is most appropriate in situations where there is much disturbed energy around.

White symbolizes purity and vitality. It reflects all colors and therefore has the effect of reflecting back whatever is sent at it. It can be very helpful where energies are being projected onto others. Its mirroring quality allows others to begin to see the effects of their thoughts and actions upon us. It is a good color to use in normal day-to-day circumstances and is often the color suggested for protection in books. However, there are some who find its energies too agitating and therefore do not get on well when using it.

Sky-blue is sometimes referred to as Madonna blue and carries a soothing, passive energy that neutralizes and harmonizes what is projected onto it. Its link with the divine feminine archetype and the quality of spiritual love gives it wide appeal. It will tend to transform and diffuse energies in a non-intrusive way. It is the natural color of those whose approach to life is more passive and gentle. However, some individuals feel that it carries a claustrophobic quality that smothers their vitality. This may be caused by difficult associations with one's mother.

These color associations have been established over a long period of time by those who have meditated upon and used color symbolism in their religious practices. These three colors are the primary protectors in the spectrum but other hues can be used, including pink and violet. These have different flavors of energy, which might attract you. The way to find out is by experimentation and noting down what you feel or sense about these qualities."

Resource: http://www.kch42.dial.pipex.com/

Some people may use an energetic reflective mirror shield as protection. It is envisioned between you and the person that you feel threatened by. It reflects back to them what they send to you.

Last but not least, you may choose to call on your spirit guides, angels or the Divine/Spirit/God to assist and protect you against psychic/energetic attacks if that fits into your belief system. They gladly will help.

Energetic Cleansing Techniques

Shower or Bath

Just as you feel cleansed and refreshed after a shower or bath, you may also use certain techniques to cleanse your energy field. Believe it or not, sometimes a water cleanse does it too. Swimming in natural bodies of water such as a waterfall, brook or the ocean can be very cleansing energetically indeed.

Sage

I like to burn white sage for smudging myself all over with the smoke of the sage. It is a Native American practice. You can sage your own energy field, or smudge physical spaces like an entire house, or room in the house, to help clear up stagnate, negative, and lower energies.

You may follow this with burning sweet grass to attract the good spirits and energy.

Hydration

I feel I need to emphasize the need of staying hydrated and the best way to do that in this case is with clear water or some herbal tea.

Nutrition

Be aware you are what you eat. Junk food affects your energy just as much as someone else's negative energy. As best as you can, try to eat a balanced diet with lots of fresh veggies and fruits. Cleaning up my diet a bit made me notice how it raised my vibrations. Limit your consumption of processed foods that contain hydrogenated oils (trans-fats), high fructose corn syrup and artificial colors and preservatives as they impact your body negatively and lower your physical and energetic vibrations. Read the food labels and pay attention to ingredients lists. Know the sources where your food comes from.

Energy Brush Technique

During my reiki training, I learned energy brush technique. It is a simple technique where you brush down with your hands first one arm then the other, then cross-wise over the torso and back and if you like down your legs. You can imagine like you are brushing off energetic dust with your hands. You can do this for your friends and family as well.

Breathing

Never underestimate the cleansing power of breath, prana! You can breathe into energy blockages and loosen them up as you breathe out. You can visualize breathing in clear brilliant air and let it circulate through your being. As you breathe out, you may visualize it as a dark cloud that washes out all the negative energy particles. Do this repeatedly until the outbreath is clear.

Detaching from Energy Drains

I mentioned above that there are humans out there that subconsciously leach off other people's energy and this can make you feel really drained. Some call them energy vampires. Some may do it unconsciously. Respected author and shaman Ted Andrews notes in his book *Psychic Protection* that we are vulnerable to energy drains through our auras, the energy field that surrounds our bodies. Andrews explains that we're "constantly giving off energy (electrical) and absorbing energy (magnetic). Every time we come in contact with another person there is an exchange of energy." Andrews is the opinion psychic vampires have an abundance of magnetic energy - which is why they draw energy away from others.

The first step is to acknowledge the situation and decide to do something about it. According to Andrews, an easy way to close off your energy circuit, thus preventing energy drains, is to "link the index finger with the thumb on each hand…then cross your feet at the ankle."

Another visualization technique a friend taught me is visualizing cutting and pulling out the energy draining cords. The energy drain cords usually attach around the energy center of the Hara, which is just about in your navel area.

You take your left arm, visualize scooping the invisible energy conductor cords up. With your right hand visualize a sword, with which you will cut and detach those energetic drainage lines. You can also visualize Archangel Michael cutting them for you. After they are cut, give the cords to Archangel Michael to take care of them. Sometimes it may be even more affective to twist and pull them out by the roots. Michael may help with this as well.

You may put your hands over the areas they attached to and heal the energy "holes" that way. You cut the cords with the intention to protect yourself from them reattaching to you. Be aware that they usually will try to reattach.

Centering and Grounding for the Indigo Child

As Indigos and lightworkers discover their skills and are sensitive to their surroundings, they easily get out of balance and stressed. The main culprits of getting stressed and out of balance are our thoughts and the story-telling mind. Too often we are so busy thinking, mostly remembering the past or planning for the future. We often forget that the actual time we do have control over, we can do something is NOW. Bringing the mind back to the present moment takes practice.

And for Indigos, on top of that come the elevated energetic sensations and psychic experiences which can be confusing and overwhelming. They make the storytelling mind and ego go haywire.

Below I am sharing some of the techniques I have found that have helped me to become grounded and centered again. One of the main exercises I have used and that has helped me to overcome anxiety and depression is mindfulness meditation.

The Power of the Breath

As you sit here and read this, you are breathing, from moment to moment without even paying attention to it. The body breathes automatically. The breath, the inhalation and exhalation of air, is a wonderful tool you carry with you everywhere you go. You can use it to come back to the present moment and finding your center again.

Here is a meditation technique used in the mindfulness practice.

Find a quiet place and sit comfortably and as erect as you can, like a helium balloon is attached to the crown of your head and gently pulling you up to help you to keep your spine straightened.

Close your eyes and sit comfortably. Take a moment to arrive in the here and now. Check in with yourself and what is going on within you. Be gentle to yourself. Bring your attention to the physical sensation of your body, and just notice. I suggest you move your attention from one to the next body part after about two breaths.

Starting at your head, your face, your neck, throat, shoulders and arms, chest, back and belly pelvis and legs, feet. Notice any sensation without judgment. You may decide to release some of tension by gently breathing into the tense areas.

As best as you can, bring your attention to the sensation of breathing. Take a moment to just observe your breath. Feel as the air enters your nostrils, how your chest and then your belly rises as you inhale and how the belly and chest fall again as you exhale. Let go of controlling your breath, just let the breath happen by itself, the body knows how to breathe. Watch it how it happens from moment to moment, with spacious awareness, meaning being a witness without trying to change or control it.

The breath is your present moment anchor point. Soon your mind will start to wander, but don't worry, that is part of the exercise process. As you notice, your mind is thinking, you just gently let go, jump off that train of thought and bring your attention back to your breath as best as you can. You are training the mind, which is like a muscle. Over time, you will get better. Do not judge yourself about thinking too much or not doing it right, this meditation practice is like a cycle. Just be, accept that where you are right now is where you are supposed to be in your practice.

You may sit as long as you feel comfortable with this practice, you may use a timer. I started with five minutes a day

Some people prefer to do some deep breathing which is great too.

Another Breathing Exercise

You may choose to visualize the air you breathe in as clear and light-filled. As it enters your body you feel it wash through you and as you exhale you visualize the air exiting as dark cloud, having cleared out any negativity.

Other centering options

Some people prefer or need something more physical to get grounded and centered. Besides my own suggestions, I am also adding some suggestions from other Indigos and lightworkers:

Go out into nature, walk, hike or meditate, preferably barefoot (not in the winter), feeling the earth under your feet. Nature has a calming effect on the mind. Most agree on that.

Hiking or walking brings the attention away from the wandering mind as we focus on every step, as each foot touches the ground. We bring our attention to the surrounding sights and sounds of nature, be it the creaking trees, singing birds, or other animals crackling through the leaves in the woods; or the sounds and sights of waves lapping against the shore when you are walking along a beach at the ocean or a lake. Not all of us have access to nature. But there are parks in the cities where you can sit under a tree or walk.

- Walk barefoot in nature if you can.
- Hug a tree! Nothing more grounding than feeling the energy of a tree trunk and its roots reaching down into the earth and branches reaching into the sky.
- Gardening. Sticking your fingers into the ground works wonders!
- Listening to music.

- Eating (I was once very spacey after an energy work exercise. Walking did not bring me back, but eating something helped to ground me again). Eat mindfully. Pay attention to the food you are eating, chew twice as much as you usually do.
- Exercise.
- Do everyday housework mindfully.

Roots visualization

One of my favorite grounding visualizations is imagining you have roots growing out of your feet right deep down into the earth, deeper and deeper. Some extend this visualization by extending it out of their crown chakra on top of the head, by imagining a ray of light connecting them to the Universe. So, light ray on top of the head, roots out of the feet.

Energy Healing

Many Indigos discover soon that they have the ability to use energy to heal other people and make them feel better. I myself have used that technique even before I became a reiki practitioner. There are many modalities that teach different energy healing techniques such as reiki, healing touch, quantum touch, etc. But there are many of us out there who never officially learned any of those techniques yet do energy healings. This chapter may be of interest to you to give you some basic tips and guidelines on energy healing.

I am of the opinion that every human being and probably some animals have the ability to channel energy for healing and direct it at another person, situation or place. Fact is that energy flows where attention and intention go.

Preparations for energy healing
- Educate yourself on the different chakra centers, subtle energy fields and their meaning when they are strong or weak
- Ask the person for permission to give energy healing. If you cannot ask in person, ask his/her higher self for permission.
- Set an intention of what you are trying to accomplish with this healing
- I recommend before you perform any energy healing to use one or more of the *energy protection* techniques in advance to make sure that you are not taking on any of the negativity or blocks from the person you are sending healing. My favorite, a white light energy bubble (see details in energy protection chapter). Set an intention through prayer to not take on any of the energy cleaned out but that it may just leave, and the Divine, the angels, spirit guides of you and the other person will take care of it.
- Connect with the Divine, angels, whatever you believe is helping you to channel the healing energy. Be aware that

the energy is not coming from you but the Cosmos. *You are tapping into the Universal Life Force Energy* that is always around us. You are merely the channel it flows through. That way the others should not be able to drain your personal reserve of energy.
- ***A word of warning:** from my own experience giving energy healing to a dying man who reminded me of my father who had died of cancer: Sometimes if there is a strong emotional attachment to the situation or person you are giving energy to, you may unconsciously allow them to tap into your energy reserve and feel very drained after the healing. This happened to me, I got burned out. Remember, that you are merely the channel, detach and let it flow. Use protection techniques before and cleansing techniques after each healing session.

Techniques: Hands-on or Distance Healing
- Do a body scan using your hands or one hand hovering over the body of the person and see where you feel the energy is off and you may focus on that spot longer than the others. For long distance healings, do it in your mind or use a teddy bear or other stuffed animal. You may feel it as warmth, tingle in your hand, twitch, maybe even something within your own body.
- You may focus your hands-on healing wherever the person wants you to, or focus on the chakra centers. Some people prefer to just hold other people's hands and thus transfer the energy.
- Be respectful of people's boundaries and where they <u>do not</u> want to be touched. Even just hovering above the body may be too much for some.

Finishing up
- If you like, do one more body scan and see if everything feels more balanced now.
- Ask the other person for feedback. "What did you feel? How are you feeling now?" Be aware it is not always obvious that the energy worked on them. Don't expect anything, just listen.

They may not notice any difference as the energy works on such a subtle level. Some may also experience what is called a "healing crisis" which means that things are getting worse before they are getting better. This does not mean you did anything bad but you may have loosened a blockage that needed to be removed in order for the real healing to take place. You can offer to do another healing later.

Detaching and Cleansing after Energy healing

This is probably one of the most important things you need to do after a healing. Make sure you **disconnect the energy cords** connecting you to the other person, to make sure that you are not getting drained. Some may unconsciously try to tap into your energy field even after the official healing is done. Ask Archangel Michael to cut the cords and take care of them. Visualize healing the spots where they detach from you. (See energy protection chapter for details).

Next, do an aura sweep, brushing off with your hands your whole body, with the intention to clean off any leftover negative energy debris from your energy fields and body. Show gratitude for any help you may have received from spirit guides, angels, etc.

You may want to cleanse the room the healing was performed in, either with sending light into all four corners or smudging with sage. You may smudge yourself with sage as well.

If there is one last tip I can give you, make sure you are receiving, every once in a while, a healing from another energy healer. Be sure to take care of yourself first before you try to help others, as a healer cannot heal if he/she is not well himself/herself.

Chapter three was written by **Sim1 Indigo,** a meditation group facilitator, Level Three Reiki Practitioner, Soul midwife, herbalist. To check more of her energy healing work, go to
http://healingsoulstice.blogspot.com/

Chapter 4

Psychic Abilities

As an Indigo it is very likely that you have already developed a few if not most of the following psychic abilities below that I will describe. The one that most Indigos share is empathy. However, the list below will describe the variety of other psychic abilities you may already have, or will soon develop in the future.

Astral Projection – Ability to leave one's body and travel in spirit to another location.

Aura Reading - Ability to see the energy fields that emanate from living beings. Psychic ability can often reveal itself through the visually seeing colors of auras.

Automatic Writing - Writing through the subconscious mind without conscious thought, or through the guidance of an outside higher intelligence.

Channeling - Associated with mediums, this is the ability to act as a channel or vessel for an outside higher intelligence.

Clairsentience - In this instance the psychic has an insight or "knowing" of and a hidden or forgotten fact.

Clairaudience – This type of ability is used to hear what is "inaudible". For example, someone with this ability could be a thousand miles way and "hear" a loved one's cry of distress.

Clairvoyance – Seeing visually. Usually confused with Precognition, this ability actually has much more in common with "Remote Viewing". True clairvoyance is not the ability to see into the future, but the psychic ability to see visually in pictures, scenes, or visions that which is hidden or far away.

Empathy – Ability to feel other people's energies, or energies of a particular environment. This is a very common gift among all Indigos.

Precognition – This is knowing the future, usually this happens mostly in dream state. However, since time is a dynamic construct, no one can ever know every detail about the future. Usually this ability refers to knowing general outcomes of specific courses of action, with occasional flashes of detailed insight.

Telepathy – The ability to communicate mind-to-mind with another person.

In order to develop each ability you must consult a person that is already experienced in the ability that you are trying to develop and learn from them personally. I suggest finding someone that you trust and already know about their backgrounds, so that you will be led in the best direction for developing your psychic skills.

The Different Types of Dreams

Many Indigos don't know this but there are 4 different classifications of dreams. For more in depth information on each classification of dreams I suggest going to your local library, Google search, or bookstore. There is a wide range of books and information on the different classification of dreams. As always use your best judgment when researching each.

Past Life Dreams

Past life dreams consist of dreams where you are recalling a past life that you once lived. Yes, in dream state you can remember the other lives that you once lived. Take a look at the common themes in the past life dreams, as indicator you are having a past life dream or not. What style of clothes are you wearing, how do people look? Are you in a city, village? What era does it look like to you?

Precognitive

A precognitive dream is a dream that you see happening that may be a future event. Usually these consist of big major events that occur to the planet such as earthquakes, tsunamis, and natural disasters like these. Sometimes there are more precognitive dreams. Precognitive dreams can also represent a more positive future event. Many people report having seen their future infant Child/Children in a precognitive dream, even before having them in physical real time reality.

Lucid Dreams

Lucid dreams are when you are aware that you are dreaming, and by thought during the lucid dream you are able to control or manipulate the dream at will. Lucid dreams are very interesting, because it gives you the feeling of complete free will during your dream.

Astral Projection

Although astral projection is not necessarily a dream, the feeling of astral projection, also known as Outer Body Experience, feels very different than a regular dream. Astral projection is the ability of your soul to leave your physical body while you are physically asleep. Your soul then can travel as far as it wants to go, both on the physical plane and the higher astral planes. If you are afraid you won't come back to your physical body, there is a silver chord that connects your spirit body and your physical body so you will come back.

Dream Weaving

Dream weaving feels like a normal dream, but a word of warning, it can be quite dangerous. When you think of someone too much during the awake state for example; there is a chance that the person will either enter your dream or you will enter their dream. I don't recommend this practice, as it can be disturbing to receive unwanted dreams from others and give out unwanted dreams to others. But, yes dream weaving is the ability to enter another person's dream, and vice versa. Usually two people who are very close to each other spiritually do some dream weaving together during sleep.

Chapter 5

Receiving Guidance – Guides and Messengers

Often Indigos feel lost in the world without proper advice on how to use their newly discovered skills. So how do you receive good guidance? Where to start? There are many ways and channels through which we may receive proper guidance which is in the highest good of all. Messages can come in many forms to us. The quickest, on the spot way of asking for guidance is through meditation and focusing on connecting with your Higher Self.

Remember that the messages may come in symbolic forms (such as objects, animals, dreams, symbols and signs, etc.) and stand for something you need to know. You will know intuitively when something is meant to be a sign or message for you, it will resonate with you. You will notice the repetition of these until you understand the message.

If you are unsure, ask if this is a sign and in the highest good of all. Listen to the inner voice in your head. Take the time to interpret the message and what it means to you. What works best for me is that I will either meditate or write about the message being delivered to me to gain clarity.

The Messengers and Guides come in many forms

Besides signs and symbols there are "beings" functioning as messengers and guides. I say beings as humans, spirit guides, angels, animals, and even plants.

Spirit guides and angels are messengers that also may come through other humans, animals or other ways described below. Sometimes, when we are clear and our energy level is balanced and our vibrations are high, we may be able to mentally hear the messages. However, it is not always easy for the guides or angels to get their message to you as we are often clouded in our consciousness with every day stress and life. It is easier for them if we are able to raise our consciousness frequency, sort of like an antenna, to receive messages via thoughts and images, or visions from them. I like to visualize sending up a white column of light through my crown. It is important to realize that the density of the third dimension makes it difficult for beings with higher frequencies to communicate with us.

Other humans can provide you with guidance from your higher self and through their own wisdom. They do not need to be necessarily spiritually awakened to do that. They may not consciously know what they are saying is a guiding message for you. What counts is that the words they are saying to you are of significance to the situation you have been asking about and that they resonate with you energetically as an important message. You may physically sense it in your heart center to be the true and kind message you needed to hear.

I have connected with many friends online and somehow through some lengthy chats; suddenly they said something and I knew I needed to hear this, that this was a message for me from my spirit guides that I did not hear otherwise, it just resonated with me. And the weirdest thing that happened if my spirit guides wanted to emphasize the importance, they would suddenly have either my or the other person's internet disconnect or the computer crash, spirit guides can have an odd sense of humor, at least this is how I experienced it.

In some herbal workshops, I have learned about how some plants can become your allies. You basically connect through your heart chakra with the energy of a plant or a tree, and communicate with the spirit or energy of the plant. One of my plant allies that used to show up on my path a lot is St. John's Wort which grows on road sides. As a medicinal plant, it helps with anxiety and depression which I used to have problems with. The yellow flower and the timing of its blooms bring the sunshine into our lives. Another one is bee balm. It has a red spikey blossom, and a sweet smell. When I connect with that flower, I can feel the sweetness of its energy and learn about how to bring sweetness into my life.

Methods of Communication:

Methods of communication can come in different forms, sometimes they are synchronistic things happening to you, or just subtle signs. I will give you a couple of examples for some subtle signs that I have experienced personally.

I am a very big admirer of the Irish author William Butler Yeats and somehow he has inspired me on my spiritual path. When I was ready to make a decision whether I want to move to the USA from my home country of Germany, some interesting synchronistic things happened around that time. One of the first signs was when I was in Ireland and visited the grave of William Butler Yeats, and when I took my camera out a leaflet from Vermont fell out from a vacation I had taken there the year before and ended up right on Yeats' grave. This resonated with me as a sign that I needed to move to Vermont. Another one was when I found a rare book by this author when I visited Vermont before I moved there. It contained an authentic stamp from a place in Ireland where William Butler Yeats used to live, the book had traveled from Ireland to Vermont and I found it at a flea market. I interpreted those signs as leading me here to experience spiritual growth. And how true this has been for me so far!

Dreams and their symbolism, you may want to write them down to help you figure out their meaning, meditate on them.

I have had a dream when I started a new job where a car and a motorcyclist were chasing me down the road. I turned around and stopped them. No one got out of the car but the motor cyclist who looked like he had stepped out of the 1950's introduced himself as my office spirit guide. I went back to work the next day more confident knowing that I could call on him to get better at my new job.

I have had many dreams where deceased family members have visited me. The most memorable one was when I met my dad who had just passed 6 months before in my dream. We were in a long hall way, and I asked him three questions. I cannot remember them all but mostly if he was all right. The last question I asked him was about details of the other side. He laughed at me in the manner I remembered him: "I don't want to talk about this now."

Thoughts and images popping into your head out of nowhere, (and sometimes repeating themselves in your head until you pay attention). Make sure it feels like it is for the *highest good, if not, ask if this is truly for the highest good.*

I experience this sometimes as a thought popping into my head with a different voice. If the message is for me, I recognize it with the resonance in my heart. If it is something I need to say to someone, sometimes the thought repeats itself in my head until I say it to the person. It usually happens while I am talking to the person. If I feel it would not be in their highest good, I do not share it. The people the message is supposed to go to then often confirm that "I helped them" but I know it was not me, I was just the messenger.

Lines that stand out in a book, parts of lyrics on the radio or lines said on TV.

I sometimes randomly open a book and look at the fifth sentence on the page for an answer. It has not worked very often for me, but it works for some people.

I was once driving home after having had a bit of an argument about something with a friend. I was very upset. As I switched on the radio, the first song had the lyrics "what did I do to deserve this" and the following "pressure, pressure, you can't handle pressure". Both of those lyrics I felt were very clear messages for me and it made me smile as it was exactly how I felt. I called my friend as soon as I got home and told her about it, we both made up and found a happy conclusion to our argument.

Another experience I had was when I had lit a candle in memory of some deceased family members, and on the way driving home the first song on the radio was "Leave a candle in the window". The lyrics were for me an acknowledgement that my family members who have passed on had received my candle greeting.

Tinnitus and ringing in your ear.

I sometimes have had my ears ring and I felt as if someone was talking about me. I have also heard during meditation something that sounded like an angelic choir.

Pay attention to the ringing. Is it a high or low pitch? Which ear is ringing? With some practice, you may be able to distinguish between a "yes" or "no" for an answer from your guides.

Finding or coming across an object that provides you symbolically with an answer (could happen during meditation). See my example above about moving to Vermont when I found the book from Ireland at a Vermont flea market.

Someone telling you something and it clicks within you that you needed to hear this as you know immediately it was a message from your guides.

Animals show up in your life telling you something, they may symbolically represent a message for you, pay attention.

Animals as Messengers and Guides

Animals can be messengers. Either the animal itself comes to guide you. Or another spirit comes to you through the animal. It is a great experience to receive messages from nature. But you must be paying attention. The more you listen to nature, the more nature will speak to you.

Often when I am contemplating an issue, a butterfly or bird visits me. I ask the animal if it is here to bring me a message. For me, if the animal flies or turns its head to my right, that is a "yes" answer. If it flies or turns its head to my left, that is a "no" answer. The direction it moves and the answers I receive are correlated with the direction my pendulum swings when I have used it.

Another example is when a bee buzzed around my hands, preventing me from cutting a piece of wood while I was building a sign board. Three times the bee stopped me from making the cut. I stopped what I was doing, sat back and thought about my design. After a moment, I re-measured the wood I was cutting, grabbed the circular saw, looked around for the bee and thanked it. The bee flew up to my face as if to say, "You're welcome," and it flew away.

The signs and messages an animal brings to you will be interpreted in a way that is meant for you to understand, trust your intuition. With practice, the animals will send you thoughts through telepathy.

How to Find Your Animal Spirit Guide Through Meditation

Get yourself into that meditative state and in your mind walk through a cave, when you come out of the cave, look around. Are you in a field? The beach? The forest? Ask to see your animal guide. If you wish, ask for your animal totem for your chakra. (Start with the root chakra the first month. The next month, ask for an animal totem for the sacral chakra. And so forth each month).

You must realize that the animal can be as big as an elephant or whale, or it can be as tiny as an insect. During one of my meditations, I kept looking around for my animal guide, not realizing that the bee I was trying to avoid was my guide. The bee buzzed around right in my face saying, "I'm Right HERE!"

When your animal spirit guide makes its appearance to you, ask for confirmation. Within the week, the animal will appear to you a few times; maybe in a dream, around your home, on television or magazines. You will notice the repetition.

The first time I tried this, it was a bear that came to me in a field during my meditation. I knew it would be unlikely for a bear to show up in my front yard but the bear found its way to confirm its identity to me. Three days after I meditated about this I was given confirmation. It started while flipping through TV channels. First, a bear stood tall in the movie "The Bear." I changed channels and another bear was on a commercial. I turned the TV off and picked up a magazine and there was another picture of a bear. Confirmation received.

Once you have received confirmation, learn about the animal's habitat, how it behaves, and its sleep patterns. What does the animal eat? How does it hunt? What animals are its predators? Honor your animal guide by learning as much as you can about its nature. Draw or hang pictures of the animal. Thank the animal for the message it brings to you.

You can find deeper insight and meanings for each animal in this book, authored by *Ted Andrews:* <u>ANIMAL SPEAK: The Spiritual and Magical Powers of Creatures Great and Small.</u>

I (Sim1) have had some amazing experiences with animal spirit guides. One time I was alone at home at night and a strange car was driving up our driveway, turning off the engines and lights. I did call the police, I was really scared. But what happened too is that I suddenly heard an owl's cry outside the window which made me feel safe, I got the message in my head that the spirit police (the owl being its messenger) were watching out for me. The car left within minutes and by the time the police came, they were gone.

During an event, a Native American Elders Gathering at Sunray in Vermont last year, one elder, a

Native Mexican Grandmother, asked all the mothers with Children to come into the talking circle and sit next to her while she was speaking. I had my baby with me. It was amazing. The Grandmother was talking about the importance of teaching the next generation about the earth and spirituality as they are our future. While she was talking, a dragonfly came and landed on my daughter's head and then right afterwards on the third eye of the Mexican Grandmother. I was not the only one who had witnessed this and it seemed to me and the others like a sign of blessing for my baby.

I want to conclude saying, stay open, stay positive, send out and receive love, and always ask for the highest good.

Synchronicity

You may have heard of the term, Synchronicity, but do you really understand what it means? Most will tell you it is a random chance of events. If you are paying attention to a higher calling then you know that there are no coincidences. Your life has taken you through twists and turns, ups and downs, gained many lessons learned, and an extensive amount of knowledge. Would you be the soul being you are without that knowledge or those lessons learned?

Everything happens for a reason. A familiar phrase that defines the way synchronicity operates. Synchronicity is responsible for the power going off; resetting your alarm clock, making you late and you arrive to your destination at a later time causing you to run into an old friend; which you would have missed had you arrived on time.

It is responsible for accidentally breaking your leg while taking a dance class, causing you to take time off and redirecting your focus to your family and deciding to take an online course for health and nutrition; which in turn, you began to share your knowledge with others. Injuries as well as having a health problem such as a cold or flu are a big clue telling you to slow down and pay attention.

Once you understand and accept the concept of synchronicity the signs are much easier to recognize. I was beginning a new life in a temporary home and about to open an account at a credit union. The first time I attempted to go there, an immense amount of traffic redirected me away from the credit union. On my second attempt, an emergency situation came up and I needed to quickly return home. On the third attempt, I was road blocked again. This time it was a literal road block due to road maintenance. I got the message; do not open an account here. Why? As it turned out, shortly after this I ended up moving away from that area and completely changed the dynamics of my life and it has been very rewarding.

Now, it is important to realize that not every aspect of life is going to put you on your path. Sometimes, other entities will interfere with those little incidences designed to rattle you to throw you off your path. How can you tell the difference? It all depends on your attitude and trusting your intuition. Do you allow yourself to get angry or frustrated over something and just give up? Or do you find another way and keep trying? If it is something you are meant to do, the path will open up. If not, your guides are letting you know that is not the way for you.

When you gracefully accept the flow of changes, keeping a positive attitude and through the direction of the Law of Attraction it can lead to some very rewarding and pleasant experiences. Choose your words, thoughts, and actions wisely. Pay attention to your surroundings, listen to what others have to say and decide for yourself what you know to be right; trust your own intuition.

Chapter 6

How to Find and Follow Your Passion as an Indigo Child

Indigos by nature are very talented. From being gifted in their psychic abilities, the arts, and other highly creative ventures. Indeed being an Indigo and having many talents is not uncommon. But, how many Indigos are actually following their passions for a living? As an Indigo Child it is increasingly difficult to find your passion, because of two reasons that I've observed and researched.

Reason # 1. In studying Indigos through extensive observation I have found that most Indigos I know are so well skilled in so many things, that they have a hard time really channeling their energy and time into 1 or 2 highly focused passions. The phrase "jack of all trades and master of none," is very common among Indigos.

Reason # 2. Indigos have a very selected and specific talent or passion, but the environment they live in with the people they are surrounded don't support that one special passion or gift they have to offer the world. The lack of support from family and friends is what prevents the

Indigo from thriving with their passion and making a living from it.

What I want to share with you first of all is that if you do have many things you are interested in as an Indigo Child that it's important to really get your focus into one or two passions that you feel most called to do, and that potentially can also help you earn a living for yourself.

Use the grounding techniques described in previous chapters to ground yourself, to tuning into one or two of the passions you are most interested in, and work on them.

If you are already gifted in one specific area, I would suggest that you continue to pursue it. I encourage you to pursue it because I know that from personal experience, if a person is consistent in pursuit of his or her passion they will make a life of success for themselves. A life of true fulfillment, joy, and abundance is granted to those that continue to pursue their passion.

Reference the previous chapter on energy protection while you are working on your passion, if you feel no one in your physical environment seems to be energetically supportive of your passion in life at the moment.

Inspired Action

Take inspired action and surround yourself with like-minded people that also share the same interests and passions as you to get some support and accountability going. A great site I recommend for this is a free site called meetup.com where you can find people within your niche that share similar interests as you. That way you gather support and share ideas to start thriving as an Indigo.

The key ingredient here is to muster up the courage within yourself to truly make what you are passionate about into a success.

Follow Divine Guidance

You do this by following divine guidance. I love this quote by Ralph Waldo Emerson:

"Once you make a decision, the universe conspires to make it happen."

The universe will reward you when you are proving to yourself and the universe that you have what it takes by the action steps you take to move forward with your passion.

Learn to trust your divine guidance. Trust that you are being guided by a higher force and allow the universe to deliver to you the events, people, and resources that will be made manifest for you once you trust in yourself and start living and working on your passion.

So what if you haven't found your passion yet. How do you find your passion? If you need some guidance in finding your passion try and experiment with some of the suggestions and tips I share below.

Baker's Ultimate Recipe for finding your passion below:

5 Steps to Finding Your Passion and Doing What You Love

1. Ask Around

You are not the only one with a passion. And you are not the only one looking. Friends and family will have spent many years trying to find out who they are. They'll be living their own dreams, enjoying their own passions, or struggling to find their way as much as you are. So why not ask them?

Give your friends a call. Send them an e-mail. Start up a conversation about hobbies, dreams, aims or goals. Your friends will probably be very happy to talk with you about the things they enjoy doing, and you might even gain some inspiration!

2. Aim for Variety

It's rare for someone to find their passion right away. Nowadays, we have so many choices that we're not likely to fall into the right place straight away. Don't let that bother you. Give many things a go. The more you try, the more chance you'll have of liking something. If you're not an active person, don't try football, tennis and running before deciding you'll never find your passion – try art, music, public speaking, charity work, DIY and gaming. You've far more chance of working out what you like.

3. Give It Time

You won't come across your passion all of a sudden. It'll take time, and it'll take effort. The world's best footballer didn't kick a ball once, and realize his life was supposed to be about the game. The world's most passionate human rights campaigner probably didn't know what they wanted to do by the time they were talking, and that next door neighbor, with five Children, didn't know everything about parenting when their first Child came along. We learn along the way. We try things out, we give things time, and we enjoy things once we've learned how to do them – but the journey can be very enjoyable, too. If something doesn't feel right at the start, keep trying for at least ten days – you might find that all it takes is a little bit of practice.

4. Volunteer Your Services

There can be no better way to find out if you're really passionate about something than to do it for someone else, without being paid or rewarded. If you think photography's for you, try standing in the rain for five hours taking photographs of someone else's wedding day. If you're certain you want to change the face of politics forever, try delivering a thousand leaflets as part of your campaign. If you can get through the exhaustion, and still love what you're doing, you're probably on the right track.

5. Say "Yes"

A top tip now: always say "yes". There are books and films about this very concept. Saying "yes'" will always lead to fantastic new experiences, and the more you experience, the more you'll learn. If a friend invites you to a party, say yes.

You might meet someone that'll have a real impact on your life. If your brother asks you to fix his computer, say yes. Even if you can't fix it, you'll probably end up learning something new. If your sister asks you to accompany her on a tandem skydive...well, you get the idea! Say "yes," and you'll be trying new things. Say "yes", and you'll be making the most of life. Say "yes", and you've a much higher chance of finding your passion and thriving!

Chapter 7

Manifest Your Desires as an Indigo Child

Manifest Your Desires

As an Indigo Child your ability to be, do, and have what you want in life comes more naturally. As Indigos understand how energy works. We are all energy beings. As an Indigo Child you understand this clearly, with your natural ability to feel the energy of other people that are around you.

We manifest into our lives what we think. Thoughts are *things* because thoughts carry an energy vibration frequency. The result of this vibration is that we radiate our energy outwards. If you are interested in not only surviving, but thriving as an Indigo Child this last chapter was designed especially for you. I will share the technique later in this chapter that will help you manifest into your reality what you truly want to be, do, and have into your life.

The wonderful thing to understand here is that the energy that you radiate or send out attracts other situations, events, persons, etc. which are in harmony with your internal energy field.

So, let's say you want to manifest your desires, which may include a new car or a new house. If you have only known lack in your life, this may be a problem for you.

Why should this be a problem? Because your internal energy field radiates "no car" or "old car", and not "new car" or "new house".

So if you try and manifest while you still have the "lack" energy field you will not succeed. The result will be frustration, anger and disappointment as I have experienced in my own life.

This has caused many people to give up saying that "manifestation" doesn't work. However as you have seen now, it's not that it doesn't work.

It is just because people don't properly understand how things work. Once you understand how things work and apply the techniques properly, you'll easily attract the things you want.

1. Manifesting is Determined in your Inner World

You manifest all the time. What you manifest in the outside world is determined to a large degree by your inner world.

The inner world includes: your feelings about yourself and the world– your thinking patterns– the often very limiting convictions about what you can or cannot do.

The outer world, on the other hand, is everything outside of yourself – including all your relationships, how much money you make, and so on.

So depending on your thoughts, convictions and feelings about yourself and the world, you either limit yourself or you manifest whatever you desire. And yes, this involves the Law of Attraction bringing opportunities and situations your way, in which the universe conspires to support you in manifesting your desires.

2. You can Change your Inner World

There are ways to change your inner world – your convictions about what is possible for you and even the way you feel about yourself can be changed. These changes will then reflect in your outer world – what you manifest through the Law of Attraction.

Often, you hear people saying that you need to think about what you desire and it will come into your life through the Law of Attraction. While changing your thoughts is an important part of the manifesting process, it is only the first part of it.

The second part is your feelings. If you think about manifesting more money, but you feel that you do not deserve more money, then those feelings (inner world) will reflect in what you manifest in the outer world.

So what you think about a desire (more money) and how you feel about having more money can be in conflict.

For powerful manifestation, your feelings and thoughts regarding what you desire should be in alignment and as free of mental and emotional blocks as possible.

There are many ways to remove mental and emotional blocks. Probably the fastest and most effective way is by knowing the law of abundance. In future book editions, we will talk more about the most common blocks in manifesting desires and what can be done to remove them.

What I've learned in my own experience is that this process below has been very beneficial to my own personal life currently at the age of 27.

From manifesting and owning a nice home, to successfully self-publishing 4 e-books, being my own boss, manifesting positive supportive relationships with amazing people, and enjoying abundance in my life…I can say the powerful process below works.

No, I am not a millionaire or drive ultra-fancy cars. But, I do live a life of freedom, and a lifestyle that suits me best at this moment, that I can honestly say I sincerely enjoy, and that I am very grateful for. I have a well-known blog and it inspires and empowers many people worldwide. This feeling of fulfillment and accomplishment in knowing I am following my passion for a living and that it is making a difference in people's lives is one of the best feelings in the world. It all started with a simple belief. It all started with the powerful process that I will unveil to you below.

The process is called **Creative Visualization**. What I've learned is that by consciously applying the process of **Creative Visualization** in my own life that the results have been a very blessed and enriched experience for me personally. I made a vow to myself that if I started using creative visualization and start seeing success with it in my life that I would teach it to others so they too can benefit from an enriched life as well.

Below is the step by step process to applying *creative visualization* in your own life. Apply this step by step process for 30 days, and see if it doesn't help the manifestation process happen for you with success in your own life. You can use this creative visualization process that I describe later to start manifesting what you want into your life in unison with the chapter of finding and following your passion in a positive and uplifting way.

Making Creative Visualization Part of Your Life

American philosopher William James once said, "Belief creates the actual fact." Of course, if you believed the world was flat, you'd be delusional, but that's not what we're talking about. Creative visualization is the underlying principle of the very commonly used word and concept, optimism. Practitioners define it as the endeavor to affect the external world with changes to internal thought.

This is not, If you build it, they will come, but rather If you think it, it will build itself. It is scientifically proven in sports that creative visualization works. So science backs up the positive results of creative visualizations with hard data to prove it works.

History and Use in Sports

First conceptualized in the US with the 19th century New Thought movement and practiced by Wallace Wattles (who also studied Hinduism), creative visualization has garnered significant scientific attention and applause in recent years. Perhaps most notable is the Soviet Russian scientific experiment that involved 4 groups of Olympic athletes, whose training schedules were changed and studied:

Group 1: 100% emphasis on physical training

Group 2: 75% emphasis on physical training with 25% emphasis on mental training

Group 3: 50% emphasis on physical training with 50% emphasis on mental training

Group 4: 25% emphasis on physical training with 75% emphasis on mental training

The Soviet experiment concluded that Group 4, the one which trained least with the body and most with the brain—using visualization techniques using all of their senses—performed the best. Strenuous visualization exercises of the mind, in this manner, acted as preludes to muscular impulses.

Benefits to Daily Life

Similarly creative visualization has been used among several athletic training circles to enhance performance. You can use this technique in your daily life, however, and not only in physical endeavors. If you have a specific goal — to behave more positively and less reactively; to add a mile to your daily jog; to feel less pain from an old injury giving you, despite therapy, chronic pain — creative visualization can be another tool in your arsenal of meaningful, positive living.

Creative Visualization in Practice

1. Situate yourself in a quiet, calm, and comfortable place, much like you would for yoga or meditation.

2. Relax. Make a conscious effort to feel individual parts leading to each other with relaxation—from your toes to your feet, your feet to your legs, your hips to your belly, etc. Focus on your breathing when your body has relaxed. You may have to make conscious efforts to stay relaxed at first, but practice makes perfect.

3. To begin the visualization process, decide what goal you wish to achieve. A better occupation? Healthier lifestyle? Start smaller than these vague, grand goals into ones you can quantify. Work your way up to broader goals as you become more adept with creative visualization and can acknowledge that it has positively affected your life.

4. Once you have a grasp on the goal you wish to achieve, picture it. Picture the object or yourself in the desirable situation as if you already had it. Do not scorn or belittle this image—treat it as a reality. Concentrate on details of this picture and try to feel it with individual parts of your body, especially if this is a physical goal. The key here is to really **feel the experience** as though it were really happening right now, not sometime later in the future, but now. The universe works on energy. The more you can **actually feel yourself as already have manifested** what you desire, the quicker you will manifest your desires.

5. Release yourself from this meditative state and go on about your day. Think of the image you conjured frequently, though. Visualize it over your morning cup of coffee or tea, during your lunch break, while lying awake in bed. Surround this image with positive energy. Like meditation or any other therapy or activity, creative visualization takes practice, dedication, earnestness, and time. Treat creative visualization as a tool on your lifelong journey, not as a pill you pop whenever you need an energy boost. You are the author of your destiny. Create consciously.

This survival guide has shown you many techniques that can be very beneficial and helpful for you as an Indigo Child. We want to leave you with hope and inspirations, to not only survive as an Indigo Child but to use your innate supernatural abilities to be your very best and thrive.

Chapter 8

Make Your Everyday Life a Meditation

One of the main complaints I hear from people about meditation is that they either do not have the time or the patience to just sit to meditate. In this day and age, we are all busy, but sometimes even five minutes in the morning, sitting up in bed and just observing the breath or sitting on the toilet or standing in the shower can be the start of a daily meditation practice. It is not a question about not having the time, but making it.

But even if you are not someone who can sit still for some time, there are ways you can make your everyday life a meditative and spiritual experience. I am structuring this topic into two sections, one with every day activities and how to make them a meditative experience, and the second one about mindfulness and human interactions.

Everyday Actions Can Be a Meditative Experience

Being with what we do at any given moment is a mindfulness meditation practice. If you are like me, your mind is constantly somewhere else, thinking of the past or planning for the future, hardly ever present where we are and what we do. As mentioned in the grounding chapter, while we sit in meditation practice, we are observing the breath as we are breathing in and out without controlling it, just watching it. And if a thought comes up, we notice it, and gently release it and bring our attention back to the physical experience of breathing. If you cannot sit still to just observe your breath, here are some suggestions on how to practice mindfulness meditation in different ways with every day things we do.

Mindful Walking and Standing

As you walk from one place to your destination, if you can, slow down a bit, and become aware of the subtle movements involved in walking.

Standing still, it starts with shifting your weight onto one leg while lifting the other, a shift in the hips, a bend in the knees, the foot touching the ground and another shift of weight, as the other heel starts lifting. Notice the expansion and contraction of your muscles.

Become aware of the ground under your feet, your breathing pattern while you walk or your arm movements, you can shift your attention between those.

Be aware of where you are, looking around you, seeing the details of buildings, plants and humans.

Smile and look at the reaction of others. If your mind wanders, as best as you can bring it back to that present moment experience. Start collecting smiles from others.

When you are standing in a line at the grocery store or somewhere else, be aware of the sensation of standing with knees slightly bent. You may choose to shift your weight from one leg to the other, observe your breath, and be aware of who is in front of you and who is behind you, and what is going on in your mind. Are you being impatient? Let it go with your out breath.

Mindful Eating

In a busy day, we usually do many things while we are eating and hardly ever are present with what we eat. We do not chew enough which causes digestive problems. First step is to not read, watch television or be on the computer while you are eating so you can bring your full attention to your experience of eating. I will illustrate how to be mindful of eating an apple.

Feel the apple with your hand, look at its colors, its skin, its dents and form and how it fits into your hands.

Smell it and see what happens in your mind and mouth.

Touch the apple with your lips and again observe what happens in your mind and mouth.

Take a bite but do not chew yet, and just explore the taste and the texture of the apple with the tongue in your mouth.

Start chewing and be aware of how the texture and the taste changes with every chew.

Chew a lot.

Once you are ready to swallow, be mindful how the bite reaches the stomach.

Try this with chocolate and you will see how this can change your eating experience into bliss!

This practice also increases the breakdown and assimilation of the nutrients actually in the body.

Other daily mindful practice ideas
- Mindful showering: feel the sensation of water on your body, temperature and all, rather than thinking about the day ahead. Change the water to cold and see how your body reacts
- Mindful driving: turn off the radio; be aware of where you are on the road, your surroundings, and the car in front and behind you. Let go of wanting to not sit in traffic but see the red brake lights as reminders to pause and breathe, to be in the moment. Be kind to your fellow travelers and do not react if someone cuts you off or takes your right of way, take a deep breath, and continue towards your destination. Follow the speed limit!
- Mindful house cleaning: When I vacuum clean, I focus on the movement of the vacuum and how I cover every inch of the floor, being aware if my mind wanders, gently bringing it back to the present activity. Cleaning the dishes is another good one,

being aware of the temperature of the water, the texture of the dish and how the stains disappear.
- Mindful cooking/making a cup of tea mindfully: This starts with the process of preparing the ingredients, boiling/baking, and then eating/drinking. With tea it is especially fun as you wait for the tea to seep and can observe the color of the hot water change and smell the essential oils.
- Mindful gardening: great opportunity to connect with nature more deeply. Just imagine weeding your garden mindfully, weed by weed, digging deep into the ground feeling the earth between your fingers. Or setting the seeds and then watching the plants grow as you nourish them. You can also do that by repotting a houseplant.

Practicing those little things can help you to be more in tune with yourself and your environment, as well as with other people.

Dance as Movement Meditation and Spiritual Practice

There are many ways to practice sensing energy or to meditate in motion. One of my favorite movement practice is dance, and the form of dance I prefer is actually called soul motion (created by Vinn Marti) and another one Five Rhythms (created by Gabrielle Roth).

Dance as a form of spiritual devotion, meditation or to evoke ecstasy has been practice in many ancient cultures and still is in many indigenous tribes. Even in Europe, the farmers used to dance to connect with the energy of mother earth in the spring, by stomping the ground, to wake it up and make it fertile.

The dance I do with a local community is not choreographed, in dance terms; you could say it is improvised. It is not a performance, more of a ritual, for the self, and sometimes with others. You listen to how your body wants to move, just let it move however it wants to, to release potential energy blocks, thoughts or emotions. Listen to the soul how it wants to move you. Dance like no one is watching. It is not a performance, it is for us.

Quieting my mind, I often just start by lying on the floor and following my breath. Then I start sensing the floor under my body, feeling the gravity of the earth embracing me. I start playing with that energy by rolling around on the floor, stretching or curling up, just connecting with the ground and my body, my muscles everything I can sense at that moment.

The music playing in the background at this point does not matter much to me, it is there to give me some guidance but the dance is my own, I am dancing intimate, centering, connecting with myself, grounding, before I take off.

The music for those kinds of dances is usually inspirational in nature, soft at the beginning, getting wild at times, and then again time to re-center. Choose a variety from New Age to pop to classic and so on. The lyrics are often inspiring and thought and intuition provoking. Sometimes the person leading the workshop (sometimes there is just a DJ playing the music) will also give some guiding ideas as to what to do next, inspirational suggestions. Such as, connecting with what is behind us and in front of us, the past and the future, and with above and below through our dance movements. I love to do that by spiraling with my arms around my body, moving my energy in the present from the past into the future.

    Once I start moving, it is fun to experiment with movement to the music, not following the melody beat by beat, but skip a beat or two or more, move slower, change the rhythm within the music, variety, and see what the body, your energy does with that, how it shifts. I sometimes watch with a soft gaze the movement of my hands and depending on the light, I can see the energy moving around my arms and hands, it is the most amazing experience. And when I widen my consciousness to see others, I can see their energies move as well.

    Aside from dancing intimate, eventually, I usually dance with another person. The dance of two flows into each other; which is the sign for an agreement to dance "in union". This is an interesting energy experience, as two heart fields merge and start to move with each other in synchronicity. It is hard to describe other than it flows and moves in waves. You may get inspired by the dance of the other, yet you remain true to your own dance, not drowning your own truth by copying another.

Eventually, there comes a time to detach and move on to another, or, to the self. This I learned to be such a valuable lesson for life, to let go and move on, not worrying about the other person but see it as the natural flow of life.

The most insightful part of this dance for me is always the pause, where I stop moving as I feel I got lost in my thoughts, and I re-center and reconnect with myself and the Divine.

We also dance as a group in community. The interesting part here is the sense of the energy of many as you expand yours but at the same time you can move away and contract your energy field to dance intimate again whenever you feel that is the right thing to do for you. Yes, it is like a wave.

There are websites where you can check for local groups in your area for Soul-motion or Five Rhythms. Sometimes there are other names like chakra dance, yoga dance. Etc. I highly recommend it as it has helped me to unite my spirituality with my physicality in the most beautiful way. Or, just turn on the music and dance at home or in the park, let the body move you and dance like no one is watching. Sense the energy within and around. I used to create an energetic field around me dancing in night clubs; it was fun to notice how people stopped bumping into me all the time.

Mindful Speech

Communication can be a spiritual practice. Words have power, transmit energy and connect you with others. Intonation and the choice of words can influence how the other person response to what you say. It starts by just being aware of how what we say impacts others. Think before you speak.

Words have energy. Their meaning and vibration influences how they are received. Let the essence of your words be filled with love, honesty, truth and understanding.

Ask yourself before you speak: Is it true? Is it helpful? Is it necessary? Is it kind?

Take a few breaths before you speak or send a message. Reread a message before sending it if it is about a delicate subject.

Words can hurt, make people defensive or lift them up and make them happy. That is the power of words. So be mindful of what you say! Misunderstandings happen because the people talking with each other come with a different decoding system from their own story. To get on the same page takes some people more effort than others. Being aware of that helps and maybe even knowing the other person's story.

Especially in the age of online chats and messaging, misunderstandings happen easily as there is no face or intonation to back up the true meaning behind the written words. Be mindful of the energy of the words that are sent; be mindful how you receive words from others versus how the sender may have meant them. These are all steps that can lead to more peace in the world overall

We sometimes say things to others that are not necessary for them to hear, so what is the motivation behind us telling them those things? Is it for the benefit of all or just for us?

Be mindful of how you react to some of the things that are said and look inside if it feels intense to find the source. Look at what triggered this reaction (meaning lashing out versus responding mindfully) within and where this came from. This may be a learned behavior trigger going as far back as our childhood.

Deep Listening

I am sure you have had those moments where you catch your mind drifting off thinking of something else while someone is talking to you. You are no longer present with them and their message. You are caught up in your thoughts. It takes a lot of effort at times to listen to someone if you feel that what this person is talking about is irrelevant to you. Your storytelling mind is telling you this is boring or this person is just wrong. The other person may sense your disinterest, and if someone has ever done this to you, you know it can be a painful experience. If you are in a meeting, a class or workshop, this often happens. We drift off. Or we judge as we disagree with something that is said.

Tips to for deep listening and being present
- What if you made a real effort to be fully present with whoever is talking to you or a group of people including you, sensing their words and their meanings, reading their body language?
- Be aware of how you understand the words said may differ from how they were meant by the sender Let go of judgment, allow others to have their own opinion. Be aware that you have a different opinion or belief system than the person you are talking to and acknowledge that everyone is entitled to their own opinion or idea. You can still tell them your opinion but make sure it is not said with the intent of judging the other person, say something, like "I see what you mean, my opinion is different but that's ok."
- Do your best to stay present with your attention to listen to what the other person is saying even if you feel this is boring or irrelevant. Look them in the eyes or if that is too hard then on their third eye while they talk.

There are some fun exercises you can practice with your friends to test your communication and listening skills. Sit back to back, one of you holding an image the other one not seeing it. The one holding the image describes what is seen in a way that the other can draw it. The same can be done with complex tinker toy structures held and the other person has to rebuild it exactly.

Mindfulness and Parenting

If you are not a parent, do these things with your young family members or neighborhood kids; consider becoming a mentor volunteer to be a positive influence on our children's lives.

As a working mother, time I get to spend with my daughter is precious. I remember how one man said at a meditation group once how he practices mindful communication skills with his kids and made an effort to be with them completely for at least one hour a day, listening to what they have to say and communicating with them on their level. Parents of younger children function as role models for their children. So I am making more of an effort to show my daughter how she can deal with her emotions without screaming and teach her ways to soothe herself (breathing). When she screams in frustration, I stay calm, acknowledge that she is angry things are not going her way and ask her to breathe and calm down. After a while, I find ways to get her attention on something else and she gets over it. Instead of reacting because things seem out of control and I am frustrated, I respond and stay in control of my own emotions.

I encourage other parents to spend as much time as you can out in nature with your kids. And play, playing is such a great way to connect with your kids in a fun way and it is educational as well! I am not talking video games; I am talking real games and playing outside. I taught my daughter how to hug a tree and the other week at the farmer's market in a park she ran off and hugged three trees without me prompting her. Nature is a great teacher and teaching your kids ways to find solace and the beauty of the divine in it early on will help them to stay connected with it as adults. Maybe create a garden together, build dirt and sand castles or a fort out of branches. It is a lot of fun to go on adventures in nature, discover all kinds of creatures and plants, talk to them and feel their energy with your kids. Listen to the sounds of nature together.

There are many games out there how you can explain spiritual concepts to kids. One of my favorite is explaining souls, energy etc. You just use water, ice cubes and let the ice cubes melt, showing how they change form. Then you boil the water and it dissipates into air. So the souls from the human body move on in other energy forms that we may not necessarily see.

Human Touch, Spirituality and Mindfulness

When we connect on a physical level with one another, it does not always mean we also connect with each other as deeply as we think. Human beings need about 12 hugs a day according to research in order to be happy and healthy. Human touch is a form of energy connection and exchange and a simple hug connects your heart field energy with that of another being. At that moment, you are influencing each other's neurological system. The hormone oxytocin is released into the bloodstream which helps a person to relax, provided that there is trust between the huggers. I am adding the trust part as many are not open to just be hugged.

Connecting On an Energetic Level

The Institute of Heartmath has done some very interesting research on the human energy field expanding from the heart. It is an electromagnetic field that extends out several feet around your body. Now that you know about this you can choose to be conscious of that field at any given moment throughout the day. When your energy actually combines with that of another, with this kind of awareness you have a new level of control over your own energy field and how you relate with others, and when to detach.

As may have mentioned before, whenever we interact with others, we connect with them energetically. Be aware of what you are sensing and learn to discern what is yours and what you may have picked up from someone else by asking yourself "is this mine?" If the answer is no, wrap it into light and love and return to sender. If it is yours, be gentle with yourself and explore it with tender awareness like a mother would help her child.

Imagine two friends or partners, male or female, are willing to completely be present with their body, mind, heart and soul when they are physically present with each other. It can be as simple as looking into each other's eyes or holding hands. You each allow the energies to merge, opening your heart in total trust to each other. You allow the divine energy flow through you by connecting not only with each other but with the divine energy. Imagine how this can deepen the connecting and spiritual experience, as you raise your vibrations to a new level combining body, mind and spirit with another human soul! It can assist you both in harmony to connect with the divine.

To sum it all up, every human interaction you have is an opportunity to integrate your spirituality, your meditation or mindfulness practice into your everyday life and to grow from that. Small acts of kindness make this world a better place and it starts with you. You start the ripple effect. It brings us one step closer to a better world. Now you just have to remember to practice.

Chapter 9

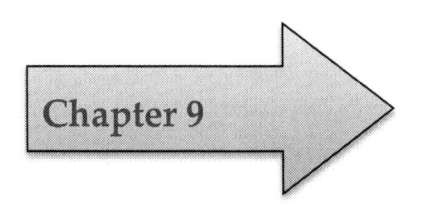

Empathy 101: A Basic Understanding of Feeling Others Emotions

Have you ever walked into a room and felt tension in the air? Have you ever become angry with someone because they were yelling at you? Have you ever felt sad, angry or happy and could not think of an obvious reason within your experience why you feel that way? Have you been in someone's presence and could feel their physical and/or emotional pain within you? Have you ever felt like crying because someone else was crying? Have you ever been hugged by someone giving you their love and felt warm and full of love? Have you ever laughed so hard that your sides were hurting because everyone else around you was laughing that hard? Congratulations, you have experienced *empathy*.

Sympathy vs. Empathy

Do not confuse being sympathetic with being empathetic; there is a difference. To be sympathetic to someone means you have a general understanding of what they are experiencing and you show them compassion, providing comfort and reassurance. To be empathetic means you feel their emotions or physical ailments within you as if it is your own, literally. Empathy is the ability to feel other people's energies, or energies of a particular environment.

Recognizing Your Empathic Ability

What I hear most from people who are aware of their empathic abilities is, "*Ugh! I can't take it! I can't stand being around all this negative energy from everyone. I've had it!*" Hold on now. Do you realize that with this attitude you are sending out and also attracting more negative vibes?

Every thought you think, every word you say, every emotion you feel and every action you take is energy. That energy goes out to others and has a direct effect on the world around you. This is not philosophy, this is science. Quantum physics is providing tangible proof that thoughts are energy. Energy cannot be destroyed, only transformed or redirected. You have it within you to transform emotional energy into a positive state. It all begins from within with your own attitude and perspective.

Controlling Your Empathy Skills

First and foremost, you must be able to recognize and take control of your own emotions. You cannot shut down your emotions, you only ignore them. What happens when an animal in a cage that has been ignored and it gets out? You feel something. Recognize it. Know it. Own it. Control it.

In any situation you find yourself, possibly feeling an overload of emotions, first ask yourself, "Do these feelings belong to me?" If the answer is, "No, these feeling are not mine," wrap them up with love and "return to sender." If the answer is yes, those are yours, allow yourself to be present with what is there and also surround those negative energies with loving light, perhaps breathing into it and releasing what no longer serves you, transforming it.

I once walked into my parents' home and within two minutes I was feeling angry. I paused for a moment, realizing that I was not angry but I was sensing the energy in the home. I wrapped up those emotions with love and returned them. I also planted my feet, grounding myself and consciously sent out positive energy through the house. I honestly cannot say if it changed the sender's mood (I like to believe it did), but those negative energies no longer affected my mood.

Knowing yourself, being your true self, is key to being able to recognize your own feelings or emotions separately from others. Once you can recognize and control your own emotions, including your outward reaction to situations, you can learn to control your empathic ability. It starts with creating a shield or your personal energy field. The armor of light or the light shield in the form of a bubble (mentioned in Chapter 3) you surround yourself with cannot be physically seen, only felt. Your energy field is your "personal space" that only those you allow to penetrate can get through.

Creating the Light Shield

You can use the technique to create a light shield bubble as described in Chapter 3, or if you would like a different way to visualize the shield, the following is a meditative exercise to build your light shield. And in time with practice, you will be able to raise your light shield with the simple snap of your fingers, or as quickly as the thought crosses your mind.

Breathe and Visualize

Calm your mind and center yourself. Inhale through your nose and exhale through your mouth; taking long deep breathes. Much like what you would do in meditation. You can do this with your eyes open or closed which ever you are most comfortable with. See the light within you, that little glow that is the essence of your soul and push that light outward. Surround yourself with your light. The color of light may vary and is your choice (see Chapter 3). You can make your light shield bubble as thick as you would like it. After doing this, pay attention to how you are feeling. I bet you are already feeling calmer and more relaxed.

The light shield can be used to control what you feel from others. It does not have to be "full shield" or "no shield." You can extend your light shield bubble out to others like reaching your hand out to touch them; all it takes is the thought. Visualize your light shield bubble extending outward, connecting to other individuals. You can receive emotions as well as send out emotions with. Be careful what kind you send out; you certainly do not want to create more negativity.

> **NOTE:** *You can choose who you connect with. You are not invading their privacy. If they do not want to be felt, they will be shielded, consciously or subconsciously. We each feel others emotions, most often without realizing it.*

Practicing With Empathy Skills

Here are a few practice exercises to help you learn how to control empathy. With these practices, you can learn to control and how to recognize where the emotions are coming from, along with sending out your own positive energies.

Practice Exercise #1 - One on One Connection

1. Center yourself, calm your mind and light shield up.
2. Choose one person and extend your light shield bubble out to them. Feel that one person's emotions. Pull your light shield in closer to you.
3. Extend your light shield bubble back out to that person and send them a "virtual hug," positive vibrations. And watch the expression on their face.
4. Pull your light shield bubble in closer to you and choose another person.

Practice Exercise #2 - Spaces and Places

1. Center yourself, calm your mind and light shield up.
2. Walk in to a public place. Push your light shield bubble outward. Fill the place with positive vibes.
3. Put a second light shield bubble up around you by finding the light within you and push it outward, keeping it close to your body.
4. Anyone who is giving off negative energies or vibrations put another light shield bubble around them with mirrors inside towards that person; their negativity will reflect back to them.

Practice Exercise #3 - Sensing Surrounding Energies

1. Center yourself, calm your mind and light shield up.

2. Stand still and focus on energies in front of you. What do you feel? Sense?
3. Focus on energies to the right. To the left. Behind you. Focus on one area at a time.
4. Practice clockwise, counterclockwise, and random directions.

Go out, practice and experiment with your discovered ability; Keeping your heart and mind in a place of joy and love will strengthen your light shield as well as affect others with your positive energy.

Using Empathy in Your Daily Life

If you realize you have the empathic skills, which I believe everyone has the capability, then you can consciously help others and raise the vibes on the planet.

Group Meditations

The whole idea of sending out positive energy is why many people get involved in group meditations. It has been proven that when a group focuses and meditates with their hearts, sending out love energy to the world, there is a positive shift in the empathic atmosphere.

Group meditations are a great way to shift the world's energy. However, what you do after the meditative session will make a greater and longer lasting impact. Many people, who participate in a group meditation, go to church or other religious gatherings (which is also a form of group meditation), get in synch with the crowd, fill the space with love; and then return to their daily life patterns with a completely different attitude.

If you find yourself screaming at your kids or siblings, yelling angrily at a driver who cut you off, or even holding a grudge against your neighbor because their tree is over your fence line, then you will be counteracting any positive energy created during a "group meditation."

Empathy in Public

Often, when I go out into public, I make a mental effort to send out good vibes. I will walk around smiling, giggling and humming under my breath, as I feel my energies spread out. By the way, smiling, laughing, singing, and dancing are a few things you can do to raise your own vibes. You can help make a difference just by keeping your own positive energy up and help to raise others.

Here is an example of what I have done with my own empathic skills:

One night we (my Love and I) went out to dinner. Near the end of our meal I was overwhelmed with emotions with a part of me that wanted to cry. I realized it was not me. I was fine; it was someone or more than one person in the restaurant. At first I looked around, connecting with different individuals, feeling their emotions. But then I decided to just "send it out" and fill the room with good vibes. I sat there quietly humming a little tune, pushing out "happy vibes" in all directions around me. My Love touched my hand and asked me if I was ok because I was so quiet. "I'm working," I told him. With him holding my hand, it was a boost of energy and I was able to send out more. When we got up to leave, I walked past one of the waitresses sensing that she was the one who wanted to cry. I wrapped her up in a "virtual hug."

Everything you do is energy. How are you affecting the world? Is it positive? Is it kind? Your attitude is YOUR CHOICE. You are in control of your thoughts, emotions and actions. What you think, say, feel and do in your everyday life is where you can truly make a difference.

Animals are naturally Empathic

Have you ever cuddled up with a dog or a cat? Have you ever felt down and your pet snuggled up with you? They feel our emotions, too. If you are paying attention, you will feel theirs. And if your connection is strong enough, you may even receive telepathic images in your mind from your pet or other animals.

Sensing Energies of Objects or Spaces

An imprint of energy is what remains long after a person has walked away or an event has taken place. Feeling an imprint of energy on an object by touching it or being in close proximity is called psychometry, in many ways, an extension of empathy. You may feel the energy of the owner of the object or possibly even layers of energy from others who have touched it. As your abilities and awareness grows, you may even "see" the history in your mind.

Sensing the imprint of energies in a space is also quite common. Have you ever walked into a room and felt strange? Almost as if you "know" what happened in that space recently. You can also send out love energy, with an energy field around these objects or spaces, transforming any negative energy to a positive.

Empathy over Distances

Empathic energies are not limited to great distances. In fact, energy can travel at any distance in only a moment's time. With the rise of communications via phone calls, text messages and social networks over the internet, we have the ability to connect with people around the world. This connection gives us optimal ways to understand others on so many levels.

Have you heard of the phrase, "Reading between the lines"? This is true in a very literal sense. Not only can you hear or read a person's words, you can feel the energy behind their words.

**If you would like a little practice with "reading between the lines" this very book you are reading at this very moment is written by three co-authors. Can you tell the difference in the writing? Do you feel the different energies pertaining to different

sections and chapters? It is ok if you do not. We honestly hope we blended the sections well together.

Reading words or listening to a voice speak is one way to connect empathically. It is very possible to connect with someone at an emotional or physical level, even from across the planet. To do this, focus on the person and pay attention to what you feel.

Several times, I have connected empathically with friends while chatting with them over the internet. When one friend had a broken leg, I was able to feel and determine which leg she had broken. Another friend did not say anything to anyone, but I sensed something was wrong. I "tapped" into her and felt some pain in my ribs on the left side. I then messaged her asking if she broke a rib recently. This friend was in complete shock with my accuracy and repeatedly asked me how I knew. I had said that I felt her; she did not believe me and equated my accuracy to random chance.

Most people will not believe that this is possible. Many will deny it. You do not need their belief so long as you believe it can be done. If your idea of having certain abilities is to show off to others, you are missing the point. You have the ability to truly understand and help others; to truly make a positive difference in the world. To selflessly make a positive difference in someone's life, is the most amazing gift you can give of yourself.

Chapter 10

Psychic Training

Chapter 4 has already described a few types of psychic abilities. The previous chapter covered Empathy; the most common ability among those who are aware. This chapter will go into a little more detail about other (but not all) psychic abilities and how to practice honing in these skills. If you are recognizing that you have unlocked some of these abilities, it is a testament to your awareness.

To begin with, it is important to understand that these gifts are not supernatural. Psychic abilities are a natural part of the human experience. Supernatural powers sounds cooler, but that could be considered egotistical; in which case, if you are proud of these abilities for the sake of showing off, your own pride will knock you down.

Physically Seeing Auras and Energy Fields

Have you ever noticed a layer of color around a person, plant, animal, or object? That would be the energy field emitting from them; and yes, even objects can have an aura, or more of an energy imprint.

The different colors will reflect different states of emotion and reflect the state of health. To say that a person's aura is a specific color is only acknowledging what their mood is at that time. Aura colors can change as emotions and health change.

If you are able to look at a person and see this layer of color or even a slight distortion in the air surrounding the person, then you are able to physically see their energy. If you are seeing a specific color no matter where you look, it is quite possible you are seeing your own aura. Some people have been able to close their eyes and see the color of their own aura through their eyelids.

To practice seeing auras:
- Have a friend stand in front of a white wall. Allow your eyes to gaze softly on the space around them, extending from their body.
- You can also try this technique with tree tops against a clear sky by softly gazing at the area around the tree. You may see a slight distortion in the air around the subject or you may see some color.
- Experiment with different lighting. Some are able to see auras or energy fields with natural light, while others can see it under luminescent lighting.
- Experiment with putting your palm facing a friend's palm, but not touching. Observe the space between the hands, moving closer and backing away. You may even feel a little tingle as the energy fields merge.

Channeling and Automatic Writing

Messages come in many forms, as mentioned in Chapter 5. One way to receive a message is through yourself; the words just come and flow out of you. There are those who claim to be channeling a message from a deceased person, extraterrestrial being, and sometimes a mythical being. Many people find comfort when an identity is attached to the message. It comes from the collective universal knowledge we are all connected to and not necessarily from a specific entity; what really matters is the message itself.

If it encourages you to tap in to your own innate inner power, provides a positive and thought provoking outlook and/or stimulates you to take action with the intent of love, then it is a good message. If it does not, move on. How? Let it go. (Refer to cleansing and protection chapter).

How do you become the conduit to receive a channeled message?
- Just start writing (or typing). Clear your mind, center yourself, and allow the pen to glide across the paper or allow your fingers to fly across the keyboard.
- If you choose to channel audibly, video yourself. Clear your mind, center yourself, and begin to speak.
- You can have a general idea of what topic to begin with or you can simply do a free-write and see what flows out.
- Somewhere deep within you, you already know the words. If you search for them, you might find them. But if you just let it flow out of you, the words will come.
- You may surprise yourself when you go back and read (or listen to) what you wrote or said. (I have often done this and thought, "Whoa where did that come from?")

Intuition and Clairsentience

Everyone at one time or another gets a "gut feeling." You know that feeling deep down within you that catches your attention when something feels wrong or right? That moment you just "know" without any explanation. You can trust that feeling; that is your *intuition* speaking to you.

If you have no other ability working for you, you have your intuition. That sense of knowing without having all the information or knowing that there is still something hidden. You may not be able to explain it entirely, but you feel it.

Clairsentience is almost the same as intuition, just a little fine-tuned. As your awareness increases, so does this sense of knowing. For some, it may be an energetic pull when facing a choice of direction. It could be ringing in the ears or goose bumps on the skin. It could be your heart beating just a little bit faster. These are some of the physical signs, which sometimes accompany this sense, but not always.

This sense of knowing is one of the most difficult to explain, as well as to describe ways to practice it. It is something only you will recognize because it is your soul speaking out to you, and you have to learn for yourself how to recognize and trust that inner voice. Learn to trust that "gut feeling" you get on occasion.

Visions: Future, Present, and Past

Psychic visions cover a wide range of sight with the third eye. You probably have experienced visions and not realize if you have bought into what movies and television have portrayed. It is not necessarily a dramatic, heart stopping, gasping, and eyes rolled back type of experience. If receiving a vision is something you are not used to, it can take you by surprise. You may notice a vision more in hindsight after you experience a déjà vu moment; remembering then you already visualized the event taking place.

Visions can be broken up into categories for the beginner (some are listed in Chapter 4), or rather for someone who is becoming aware. With practice, experience, and increased awareness, you may come to realize that the different types of visions overlap, blend together, and work with other abilities.

There are several types of visions (including but not limited to): *premonition, precognition, clairvoyance, remote viewing, retrocognition, and psychometry.* With any type, vision is subjective and can only be considered truth if you are able to receive some form of confirmation.

Premonition and Precognition – Future Sight

One misconceived notion about future sight is that it is certain; and when the events fail to match a future vision, it is thought the psychic is a fraud. The future is NOT set. There are many variables that can redirect the outcome. Any future type vision is only one of many possibilities.

What this type of sight can provide is direction. Your inner soul may show you anything from a glimpse to a full played out movie in the mind of what could be. The subconscious mind has already mapped out possible futures. The conscious mind recognizes pieces through premonitions or precognitions. When you connect the conscious with the subconscious, and know that you create the future you focus on, you have the ability to change the vision.
To enhance this ability, and to apply the Law of Attraction (LOA), practice visualization.

- When you are beginning a project, see the progress and end result.

- Any worry may cause undesired results. You can use this to your advantage by seeing the possibility and correct any issues.
- The bigger the picture, or the more global the vision, the more variables there are to affect the outcome (i.e. people, climate changes, etc.)
- You have the ability to direct the outcome of YOUR world, by what you focus on.

Clairvoyance and Remote Viewing – Present Sight

Being able to see things in the present time without having it directly in front of you is an ability shared by many. It is also not uncommon to include other thought processes in this visual ability. You pick up clues from other sources using your intuition and sometimes even logical thinking or memory. All of which are using your mind.

There are ways to strengthen this ability by exercising your mind.
- Solve game puzzles of all sorts; crosswords, word searches, logic, pictures, etc. Strengthen your problem solving skills.
- Enhance your mental imagery by noticing the details around you.
- Take a mental walk through your home. In your mind, open drawers, cupboards, closets, and boxes. You can verify what you "see" and strengthen this ability.
- Take a mental walk through other places. Compare your memory to what it is now.
- Have a friend put something in a box. Practice mentally looking inside the box.

- When practicing a remote viewing exercise, trust what you are drawn to.

Retrocognition and Psychometry – Past Sight

Memory plays an important part of past visions. However, every time a memory is recalled, the mind will change the details. Some past memories go beyond the present life time. Many have claimed the ability to look in to past life records, also call Akashic records. This cannot be denied nor confirmed. You may be able to recall your own past, and you may be able to look in to the past of others.

You may get a past vision when your energy matches that of another time. For instance, during a traumatic incident, an exhilarating moment, or even during the throws of passion you may recall or receive a vision of a similar time. The deeper you become mindful of the moment, being your true self, the clearer the vision may be. In some cases, your mind will interpret it to be in the now with all of your physical senses registering the details, making it incredibly realistic for you.

With *psychometry*, visions may come through an object. You may feel specific emotions when touching an object, traces of energy that remain. You may also receive a visual history of the object. This can also be done with photos; connecting with the object in the photo as if it is directly in front of you. *Psychometry* greatly overlaps with *empathy*. The object has taken on the energy of its surroundings and owners that you pick up on. You can pick up on such energy in rooms as well, energetic imprints, remnants of the history.

Connecting with, or remembering part of the past has been helpful for some and harmful for others. Some say recalling a past memory is useful to understand issues in your current life. It is important to understand, these issues cannot be magically erased. The only way to clear your past is to learn your lessons, work through your emotions, and rebuild yourself in the present.

Some things are meant to be forgotten. You will remember what you are supposed to remember, and at the time you need to recall it. Truthfully, there is rarely a way to confirm a past vision from another time. The vision will come to you when you need to understand something or learn a lesson.

Life lessons only repeat until you learn how to change the outcome. With every new understanding, you expand your knowledge and have the opportunity to create a new way. Trust your instincts if you choose to delve into your own past. Allow it to develop naturally. If you are interested in enhancing this ability, exercise your imagination and your ability to see images in your mind.

Chapter 11

Raising and Mentoring New Paradigm Kids

Many indigo adults may be parents, teachers or mentors and due to their own level of consciousness more aware than the rest of the world of the new children that come to the world with a higher awareness and often amazing psychic skills. I am writing this chapter to call you all to action to help those kids to remain in this high vibration of love, peace and higher consciousness throughout their childhood into adulthood. These kids are our future leaders and as indigos and trail blazers it is our responsibility to create a better world, and show them how to live a conscious life that shows respect to the earth and all beings.

You do not need to be a parent or teacher to mentor those kids. You may have a great connection with a younger kid from your neighborhood, or a sibling or other family member. It is best to first just observe, and just see what you get.

Recognizing Abilities in Others

When you notice a child that has any form of psychic skills ease into the conversation of psychic skills, by asking them questions about what they experience or telling them what you have experienced. An example is if you see a child looking into a corner or talking to an invisible being, or if the child tells you about a past life experience, just ask questions. You can also make a game out of doing energy healing or even practicing meditation or telepathy. You can practice skills with them if they are open to it. Be a big brother or big sister to someone whose family does not understand. But don't push them to do something they don't want to do. Just offer them an open mind and if they ask guidance.

I have sat down with my daughter since she has been 2 ½ years old for short meditations. I usually let her choose a couple of my crystals to hold and look at. She crosses her legs as we sit either across from each other or she sits in my lap. I have shown her how to breathe deeply and chant OM. None of the sits last longer than a few minutes. She now is 3 ½ and often asks me now if I want to go and meditate.

We hug trees and listen to the sounds of nature outside and watch the bugs. She has helped me do playful energy healings as I showed her how to do it. Since she has been a baby, she has been an empath, often getting easily overwhelmed by other people's emotions. Whenever she meets new people, she scans their energy from head to toe, and I can tell if she does not like someone. She has shot a ball of energy at Mama Indigo when she was visiting us.

One father told me about his old soul son and the amazing things he talks to him about, he can read his parents' minds and knew for example before they told him when his mother was pregnant again. He knows details about information that they have no idea where he gets it from. There are so many of those amazing kids out there, we just have to keep an open mind.

Spirits and Entities

My daughter has described to me beings that she sees that I cannot see. This started very early and she had a hard time putting into words what she saw, the first being was a spirit cat. I do not see spirits, I mostly sense them. It is important if we cannot detect or see what our children see to not discount them but instead play along and ask them questions.

Kids usually tell the person they trust most about any unusual experiences such as seeing a ghost or seeing someone's energy.

A parent who wishes to stay anonymous shared the story of her eight-years-old son that I will call for convenience Tyler (not his real name). When she was pregnant with him, his father was murdered. She says that the way Tyler talks, and acts, is often way too mature for his age, a sign that he is an old soul. He sees spirits in their house, one a boy sitting in the corner that he often communicates with and then a woman that runs away. They do live close to a cemetery.

When he goes out, he tells his mother, he sees energy colors around people and spirits in other places. Just recently Tyler has told his mother that there is a male spirit attached to and around her. Upon asking some more questions, she determined it was Tyler's dad that he had never met and was killed while she was pregnant. The spirit told Tyler that he was not sure why he was still here but that he felt he had to be here. Upon asking some more questions, the mother told me that she was in such denial about the death of her partner and father of Tyler that she had asked his spirit to stay with her, so he just did. I suggested that they do a family memorial ritual for this spirit as well as go and see a grief counselor to process the traumatic events surrounding the death of Tyler's death. I continue being available to her to support her with the psychic experiences Tyler has.

I have run into some kids and just by looking into their eyes I could tell they are old souls. I have talked to some parents who have told me they fear that what their child tells them is just fantasy, and that they have no control or cannot protect them from bad energies or spirits. You do have the tools, you just teach them to your children about energy protection.

An example is if they child talks to spirits, and the spirits tell the child to do things that are bad, or scare the child, tell the child that it can say "No" to the spirit. You can make a magic wand together with a crystal on the tip and charge it with special energy to help the child to banish the unwanted beings. Teach your child to say Mama Indigo's phrase: *"I am love. I am light. I am one too strong to fight! Now, shoo."* (It only takes a small flick of the wrist to shoo away negativity). Have them say this phrase while laughing for best results.

For kids that are too young to understand their own protection, I recommend using tools, or protective crystals and put them under the bed; such as black tourmaline, snowflake obsidian, rose quartz, and clear crystal. I put a dream catcher over my daughter's bed and have created a protective energy field around her. Tools are not necessary but can be useful to direct the focus of your energy.

Nutrition
Aside from teaching our kids non-judgment, I also would like to say a word about diet. As a reiki teacher, I often recommend to students to reduce their sugar and coffee intake and eat more veggies and fruit instead of chips or chocolate and other processed food. For kids, veggies are not very appetizing but they can be hidden in delicious fruit smoothies or blended into pasta sauce. It is my experience that consuming less processed food and processed sugar helps my energy to be higher and feel more balanced and thus my psychic skills are more available to me.

Integrating and Encouraging Higher Consciousness

Our current school systems are mostly not very supportive in fostering higher consciousness in our kids but there are people out there planting seeds to create programs. There are schools that integrate meditation and social consciousness all across the country. Teaching kids outside of the education system is a growing concept. After school programs and workshops, peer play groups with fun games, and support groups for parents of psychic kids are available in some areas.

So aside on working on your own skills, I encourage you to use what you have learned and share this with others, especially the younger generation. Show them they are not alone, they don't have to hide just because their family or peers don't understand. We doubted ourselves when we were kids as our parents downplayed what we experienced. You can give those kids a chance, if you notice one being different, show them they are not alone, listen, encourage, and be a mentor.

Chapter 12

This Is Only the Beginning

Intention is the defining line. It is a fine balance between humility and arrogance. It is a matter of absolutely believing in you without boasting about yourself or getting too attached to a specific outcome of what you desire to manifest. Your intentions will determine the direction your energy flows. How you identify yourself, recognize your abilities, and how you use your abilities in the world will create your path.

Identity

The human language, regions and beliefs have created so many different labels to define us. Between nationality, race, gender, sexual preference, generations, politics, religions, zodiacs, professions and level of consciousness, the human race has divided. Do you allow the label to define you or do you define the label? The only "label" that is truly yours is your own name; the rest are simply ideas.

Many of you reading this consider yourself an Indigo, or you know someone that is Indigo or Crystal, Rainbow, Starseed, Lightworker, etc... These are all just labels; humans like labels. It is the label that brings you to others with similar ideas and beliefs. No one is less than or better than others just because they are aware of things that others might not be aware of. We are all the same with the same potential. We all have free will as to how much we open ourselves up to new levels of consciousness. Everyone has the capability of connecting with the higher self, as long as they are paying attention.

Supernatural or Natural?

Everyone is capable of reaching a higher consciousness. Everyone is capable of tapping into their most innate abilities that we perceive as psychic or gifted. Just as some people have a more natural ability to run like the wind, calculate complex mathematic equations in their head, or compose a symphony, there are some who have a natural intuitive ability.

With all of these abilities, it really is not necessary to rely on a "professional" for readings. You are more than capable of opening up your awareness and unlocking what many consider to be gifts. Again, this is part of the human experience and becoming more common; not because more people are born with these abilities, but because the concept has become more accepting and widely spread.

Whether you have gut feelings (intuition) or psychic visions, empathic senses, aura reading, telepathy, telekinesis, astral projection, clairsentience, clairvoyance, clairaudience, psychometry, channeling, remote viewing, or many other "supernatural" abilities; you should remember that these are NOT supernatural. Nor do these abilities work separately. The abilities are a natural part of you; a natural human ability.

One misconception is that there is one way of experiencing some of these abilities. There is no one way; it is different for everyone. Some of the techniques given here may work for you. Remember that these are *only suggestions and nothing is absolute*. You have the choice to find your way. These abilities are not separate either. Through experience, you eventually realize that it all overlaps and work together. How is that? It is quite simple.

It begins from within you, at your center; the core of your soul. Everything outside of your center is an extension of you. Your mind will interpret your perception in ways that will make sense for you. The greater the awareness, the more you will understand how it all fits together.

The Core Equation

I am coining this term "*The Core Equation*" to give you an understanding of what I am attempting to describe here. It is a trinity that makes up the core of your being; thought, emotion, and action -or- your mind, your spirit, and your physical body. Ancient symbols have been used to describe the relation for this trinity; such as the triskelion, the triquetra, and the trinity knot. Allow me to break the relationship down for you:

- *Thought (mind)* — The mind has extraordinary abilities. It works consciously and subconsciously. We use our thoughts to learn new things, to remember the past, to make decisions for the future, to move through the present, and when we dream, the mind reveals our deeper thoughts. When we consider our values, we use thought to guide us. Our emotions can have a direct effect on the thoughts we have, however, we do have the ability to override what we feel and use our thought to redirect our choices.

- *Emotion (spirit)* — There are only two true emotions: love and fear; all other emotions extend from these two. Happiness, joy, excitement, content, etc. are extensions of love. Anger, hatred, frustration, worry, etc. are extensions of fear. We are born with love; fear is learned. Humans are naturally compassionate. It is when we are introduced to our current world stimuli, we learn to judge and begin to fear what we do not understand. The more we fear, the further away we get from being who we truly are. Our natural state of being is love, and that love is expressed into the physical world through happiness, peacefulness, kindness and compassion. With this, to find your way back to the core of your being you must find the love within you
- *Action (body)* — The physical body is the vehicle we use to move through our life. Some of our actions are voluntary, some are involuntary. Our conscious thoughts become a physical action when we make a decision. Our emotions are expressed physically

through actions. For instance, a tantrum is a physical response to anger and laughter is a physical response to joy. Without the physical body, the energy created by our thoughts and emotions would simply drift around the universe.

- *The True Self* — The trinity between the three (mind-spirit-body) is the makeup of our being. If any one of these pieces of the core equation is missing or does not match the other two, you are not being true to yourself. When these three work together in harmony, you are being the true self. When you match your thoughts, emotions, and actions, you will have connected to the core of your being; the authentic self.

When you make the choice to use your mind to focus on positive perspectives, using those good values as a guide, to direct your emotions to the various extensions of love, and take actions that match what you think and feel, you will not only find yourself in a much more peaceful state of being, you will be driven by a passion that becomes an unstoppable force. You will discover a world that will open up for you in magical ways.

Be the Master of You

When you learn to appreciate what you have, then you will begin to deserve more. This life is yours to control. Every intention you set is energy in motion. Every thought you have, every emotion you feel, every action you take (mind, spirit and body) determines which direction you choose to focus your life's path. Your intention is the tipping point of the direction of flow for the energy you send out with your thoughts, emotions, and actions.

Control your mind, match your thoughts and emotions to your actions, and with a positive attitude and perspective, you are the master of YOU. When you match your thoughts and emotions to your actions, what you attract to you will return faster. There is nothing wrong with feeling negativity. The difference comes when you choose to not act out with that energy. Balance out your negative thoughts and emotions with positive ones, and know when to take some time to retreat and go within to release, relax, rejuvenate and heal to make room for a fresh new positive outlook on life.

Trust your senses, let go of the labels and be your true authentic self, in ALL aspects of your life. Own up to your responsibilities and develop your character with integrity. Be love with kindness and compassion for all beings. Hold an attitude of gratitude and you will discover and walk YOUR path.

Helping Humanity

Now that you have discovered these abilities within you, and most likely you are still discovering the unlimited capabilities, what are you doing with your life? How are you affecting those around you? Is it helpful? Is it kind?

Some people are likely to open up to you and tell you their life story because they just sense you are a good listener and helper by nature. Let them talk, tell their story and try as best you can to stay present with compassion and without judgment. Remember, you can be a guide post and point the direction of change if you feel they are on the wrong path but you cannot drag them along the right one. Sometimes the other person has to walk their path alone. If it is difficult for you to let go of wanting to help, then there is an issue within you that needs your attention.

Can you imagine what the world would be like if everyone found their true self, and lived a life with love, kindness and compassion? I know it is a long shot, but certainly not impossible. It begins with you.

You are a unique piece of the universal consciousness.
Your authenticity is appreciated.

About the Authors

Baker's Bio

Baker Jacinto is a full-time 28-year-old Blogger at http://www.bakerthebrand.com – a well-known spirituality blog that inspires and empowers individuals to living the life of their dreams from the inside-out. He has written four self-published books in the areas of spirituality and self-help. His life mission is to inspire and make a difference in the world by being of service to humanity in the most authentic manner possible.

Growing up, Baker felt that he had to hide his talents because they were not fully developed yet. At the same time, he also felt that the kind of philosophies and ideas that he had adopted in his life were ahead of its time. It was hard to express this to his friends because a lot of them were into the party scene. He, however, felt a lot more spiritual inside. Growing up he could easily feel and sense the energies of people and environments around him.

To escape the city life of Los Angeles, California, Baker moved to a more peaceful city in Arizona by himself. Baker has the calling to influence the world in a positive way. The topics that he writes about include abundance, awareness, inspiration, passion, success, vibration, energy, and poetry. He is not only an expert on the Law of Attraction, but also a poet of life. He has since moved from Arizona back to California to teach about the shift in consciousness that is currently happening on our planet.

Baker passionately writes about the shift in consciousness that will bring about a spiritual revolution on our planet in the near future. His emphasis is on applying the law of attraction with the new positive energy that is emerging on this planet to inspire and empower indigo children to realize their dreams. Baker believes that on an energetic level on this planet we currently are living in exciting times, and that when each person shines their true light from within, they begin to live an authentic life far beyond their wildest dreams.

Mama Indigo's Bio

Mama Indigo was given her name after spending months in public forums, guiding and encouraging others who identified themselves as Indigo. Rather than pointing people on a set path like many "spiritual guides," she prefers to support others in finding their own way much like a mother with her children. Her true identity is a mystery, albeit one that can be solved should one pick up on subtle hints left for the astute observer.

Born under Sagittarius, Mama Indigo draws from her fire sign a direct and honest (sometimes brutally so) approach and eschews tact and coddling; this applies to both her criticism and encouragement. Many have, at first, found themselves offended by her straightforward manner only to find an appreciation for her once they get past the initial shock. As a self-taught digital graphic artist, she continually advances this book's message through social media and draws in those in need of guidance.

In her daily life, Mama Indigo teaches martial arts to local children. Holding a black belt in Kenpo Karate with influences from several other styles, she uses her teaching method (just as straightforward in person as it is online) to help her students develop not only the ability to defend themselves and others but also the confidence to excel in school and in life. Her goal, along with continuing to grow as a martial artist, is to see her students and those she guides to exceed her own abilities and go on to teach younger generations.

To read more from Mama Indigo, visit her blog at http://mamaindigo.blogspot.com

Sim1's Bio

Sim1 Indigo is a Reiki Master Teacher, a mother, intuitive coach, herbalist, and soul midwife/energy healer.

As a child, she always felt different. She had several "invisible" friends and used to be an outsider in high school. She never liked church very much, but she felt God everywhere around her in nature. She apprenticed with Rosemary Gladstar in 2005, the mother of herbalism, who taught her the use of medicinal herbs. During Gladstar's workshops, Sim1 learned what she had known intuitively since she was a child, that plant spirits and earth spirits do exist and are very powerful tools for healing and grounding.

After Sim1 moved from Germany to Vermont, she started working as a receptionist at a local college and discovered her passion for mindfulness meditation. She has been teaching mindfulness meditation techniques to college students at this college for more than 10 years. In 2014, she took a workshop with Child Light Yoga to teach yoga and meditation to kids and is developing child-friendly meditation and Reiki workshops locally as well as mindful parenting workshops. She has started to work with parents of psychic kids to assist them supporting their child's confidence and to help their children to feel safe with their enhanced perceptions and sensitivities.

Sim1 has shown many people how to listen to their soul's voice over the years, finding their unique life path and shedding old beliefs and templates that no longer serve them. Sim1 has published various articles in magazines, including an article about "Mindfulness on Campus" in the magazine Mindfulness Bell as well as an article about Giving Reiki to a dying friend in Everchanging Magazine.

She shares her insights on her blog
http://healingsoulstice.blogspot.com

Made in the USA
Lexington, KY
13 June 2016